Tolerance
Affection
Clarity
Cooperation
Faith
Friendship
Love in Motion
Understanding
Dignity
Delicacy
Happiness
Empathy

PERSONAL INFORMATION

NAME

ADDRESS

HOME TELEPHONE   MOBILE

E-MAIL

BUSINESS ADDRESS

TELEPHONE

FAX

E-MAIL

WEBSITE

DOCTOR   TELEPHONE

BLOOD TYPE   RH   ALLERGIES

VACCINES   VALID UNTIL

VACCINES   VALID UNTIL

VACCINES   VALID UNTIL

IDENTITY CARD NO.   VALID UNTIL

PASSPORT   VALID UNTIL

ISSUED ON

VISA   VALID UNTIL

VISA   VALID UNTIL

DRIVER'S LICENSE   VALID UNTIL

CAR REGISTRATION NO.

MOTORCYCLE REGISTRATION NO.

BANK ACCOUNT NO.

ORGAN DONOR: YES ☐   NO ☐

MEDICAL INSURANCE COMPANY

TRAVEL INSURANCE

IN CASE OF ACCIDENT PLEASE NOTIFY

NAME

ADDRESS   TELEPHONE

PAULO COELHO

FRIENDSHIP

Day Planner
2017

Vintage International
Vintage Books
A Division of Penguin Random House LLC
New York

FRIENDSHIP

You succeeded in gaining respect for your work
because you did not work only to survive,
but to demonstrate your love for others.

MANUSCRIPT FOUND IN ACCRA

2017

JANUARY

S	M	T	W	T	F	S
1	**1**	**2**	3	4	5	6	7
2	**8**	9	10	11	12	13	14
3	**15**	**16**	17	18	19	20	21
4	**22**	23	24	25	26	27	28
5	**29**	30	31				

1   New Year's Day
16   Martin Luther King Day

FEBRUARY

S	M	T	W	T	F	S
5				1	2	3	4
6	**5**	6	7	8	9	10	11
7	**12**	13	14	15	16	17	18
8	**19**	**20**	21	22	23	24	25
9	**26**	27	28				

14   Valentine's Day
20   Presidents Day

MARCH

S	M	T	W	T	F	S
9				1	2	3	4
10	**5**	6	7	8	9	10	11
11	**12**	13	14	15	16	17	18
12	**19**	20	21	22	23	24	25
13	**26**	27	28	29	30	31	

APRIL

S	M	T	W	T	F	S
13							1
14	**2**	3	4	5	6	7	8
15	**9**	10	11	12	13	**14**	15
16	**16**	17	18	19	20	21	22
17	**23**	24	25	26	27	28	29
18	**30**						

14   Good Friday
16   Easter Sunday

MAY

S	M	T	W	T	F	S
18		1	2	3	4	5	6
19	**7**	8	9	10	11	12	13
20	**14**	15	16	17	18	19	20
21	**21**	22	23	24	25	26	27
22	**28**	**29**	30	31			

14   Mother's Day
29   Memorial Day

JUNE

S	M	T	W	T	F	S
22					1	2	3
23	**4**	5	6	7	8	9	10
24	**11**	12	13	14	15	16	17
25	**18**	19	20	21	22	23	24
26	**25**	26	27	28	29	30	

18   Father's Day

JULY

S	M	T	W	T	F	S
26							1
27	**2**	3	**4**	5	6	7	8
28	**9**	10	11	12	13	14	15
29	**16**	17	18	19	20	21	22
30	**23**	24	25	26	27	28	29
31	**30**	31					

4   Independence Day

AUGUST

S	M	T	W	T	F	S
31			1	2	3	4	5
32	**6**	7	8	9	10	11	12
33	**13**	14	15	16	17	18	19
34	**20**	21	22	23	24	25	26
35	**27**	28	29	30	31		

SEPTEMBER

S	M	T	W	T	F	S
35						1	2
36	**3**	**4**	5	6	7	8	9
37	**10**	11	12	13	14	15	16
38	**17**	18	19	20	21	22	23
39	**24**	25	26	27	28	29	30

4   Labor Day

OCTOBER

S	M	T	W	T	F	S
40	**1**	2	3	4	5	6	7
41	**8**	**9**	10	11	12	13	14
42	**15**	16	17	18	19	20	21
43	**22**	23	24	25	26	27	28
44	**29**	30	31				

9   Columbus Day
31   Halloween

NOVEMBER

S	M	T	W	T	F	S
44				1	2	3	4
45	**5**	6	7	8	9	**10**	**11**
46	**12**	13	14	15	16	17	18
47	**19**	20	21	22	**23**	24	25
48	**26**	27	28	29	30		

11   Veteran's Day
23   Thanksgiving Day

DECEMBER

S	M	T	W	T	F	S
48						1	2
49	**3**	4	5	6	7	8	9
50	**10**	11	12	13	14	15	16
51	**17**	18	19	20	21	22	23
52	**24**	**25**	26	27	28	29	30
53	**31**						

25   Christmas Day

2018

JANUARY

S	M	T	W	T	F	S
1		1	2	3	4	5	6
2	7	8	9	10	11	12	13
3	14	15	16	17	18	19	20
4	21	22	23	24	25	26	27
5	28	29	30	31			

1 New Year's Day
16 Martin Luther King Day

FEBRUARY

S	M	T	W	T	F	S
5					1	2	3
6	4	5	6	7	8	9	10
7	11	12	13	14	15	16	17
8	18	19	20	21	22	23	24
9	25	26	27	28			

14 Valentine's Day
19 Presidents Day

MARCH

S	M	T	W	T	F	S
9					1	2	3
10	4	5	6	7	8	9	10
11	11	12	13	14	15	16	17
12	18	19	20	21	22	23	24
13	25	26	27	28	29	30	31

30 Good Friday

APRIL

S	M	T	W	T	F	S
14	1	2	3	4	5	6	7
15	8	9	10	11	12	13	14
16	15	16	17	18	19	20	21
17	22	23	24	25	26	27	28
18	29	30					

1 Easter Sunday

MAY

S	M	T	W	T	F	S
18			1	2	3	4	5
19	6	7	8	9	10	11	12
20	13	14	15	16	17	18	19
21	20	21	22	23	24	25	26
22	27	28	29	30	31		

13 Mother's Day
28 Memorial Day

JUNE

S	M	T	W	T	F	S
22						1	2
23	3	4	5	6	7	8	9
24	10	11	12	13	14	15	16
25	17	18	19	20	21	22	23
26	24	25	26	27	28	29	30

17 Father's Day

JULY

S	M	T	W	T	F	S
27	1	2	3	4	5	6	7
28	8	9	10	11	12	13	14
29	15	16	17	18	19	20	21
30	22	23	24	25	26	27	28
31	29	30	31				

4 Independence Day

AUGUST

S	M	T	W	T	F	S
31				1	2	3	4
32	5	6	7	8	9	10	11
33	12	13	14	15	16	17	18
34	19	20	21	22	23	24	25
35	26	27	28	29	30	31	

SEPTEMBER

S	M	T	W	T	F	S
35							1
36	2	3	4	5	6	7	8
37	9	10	11	12	13	14	15
38	16	17	18	19	20	21	22
39	23	24	25	26	27	28	29
40	30						

3 Labor Day

OCTOBER

S	M	T	W	T	F	S
40		1	2	3	4	5	6
41	7	8	9	10	11	12	13
42	14	15	16	17	18	19	20
43	21	22	23	24	25	26	27
44	28	29	30	31			

8 Columbus Day
31 Halloween

NOVEMBER

S	M	T	W	T	F	S
44					1	2	3
45	4	5	6	7	8	9	10
46	11	12	13	14	15	16	17
47	18	19	20	21	22	23	24
48	25	26	27	28	29	30	

11 Veteran's Day
22 Thanksgiving Day

DECEMBER

S	M	T	W	T	F	S
48							1
49	2	3	4	5	6	7	8
50	9	10	11	12	13	14	15
51	16	17	18	19	20	21	22
52	23	24	25	26	27	28	29
1	30	31					

25 Christmas Day

2017 YEAR PLANNER

JANUARY

S	**1**
M	2
T	3
W	4
T	5
F	6
S	7
S	**8**
M	9
T	10
W	11
T	12
F	13
S	14
S	**15**
M	16
T	17
W	18
T	19
F	20
S	21
S	**22**
M	23
T	24
W	25
T	26
F	27
S	28
S	**29**
M	30
T	31

FEBRUARY

W	1
T	2
F	3
S	4
S	**5**
M	6
T	7
W	8
T	9
F	10
S	11
S	**12**
M	13
T	14
W	15
T	16
F	17
S	18
S	**19**
M	20
T	21
W	22
T	23
F	24
S	25
S	**26**
M	27
T	28

MARCH

W	1
T	2
F	3
S	4
S	**5**
M	6
T	7
W	8
T	9
F	10
S	11
S	**12**
M	13
T	14
W	15
T	16
F	17
S	18
S	**19**
M	20
T	21
W	22
T	23
F	24
S	25
S	**26**
M	27
T	28
W	29
T	30
F	31

APRIL			
S	1		
S	**2**		
M	3	◑	
T	4		
W	5		
T	6		
F	7		
S	8		
S	**9**		
M	10		
T	11	○	
W	12		
T	13		
F	14		
S	15		
S	**16**		
M	17		
T	18		
W	19	◐	
T	20		
F	21		
S	22		
S	**23**		
M	24		
T	25		
W	26	●	
T	27		
F	28		
S	29		
S	**30**		

MAY			
M	1		
T	2	◐	
W	3		
T	4		
F	5		
S	6		
S	**7**		
M	8		
T	9		
W	10	○	
T	11		
F	12		
S	13		
S	**14**		
M	15		
T	16		
W	17		
T	18	◐	
F	19		
S	20		
S	**21**		
M	22		
T	23		
W	24		
T	25	●	
F	26		
S	27		
S	**28**		
M	29		
T	30		
W	31		

JUNE			
T	1	◑	
F	2		
S	3		
S	**4**		
M	5		
T	6		
W	7		
T	8		
F	9	○	
S	10		
S	**11**		
M	12		
T	13		
W	14		
T	15		
F	16		
S	17	◐	
S	**18**		
M	19		
T	20		
W	21		
T	22		
F	23	●	
S	24		
S	**25**		
M	26		
T	27		
W	28		
T	29		
F	30	◑	

2017 YEAR PLANNER

JULY		
S	1	
S	**2**	
M	3	
T	4	
W	5	
T	6	
F	7	
S	8	
S	**9**	○
M	10	
T	11	
W	12	
T	13	
F	14	
S	15	
S	**16**	◑
M	17	
T	18	
W	19	
T	20	
F	21	
S	22	
S	**23**	●
M	24	
T	25	
W	26	
T	27	
F	28	
S	29	
S	**30**	◐
M	31	

AUGUST		
T	1	
W	2	
T	3	
F	4	
S	5	
S	**6**	
M	7	○
T	8	
W	9	
T	10	
F	11	
S	12	
S	**13**	
M	14	◑
T	15	
W	16	
T	17	
F	18	
S	19	
S	**20**	
M	21	●
T	22	
W	23	
T	24	
F	25	
S	26	
S	**27**	
M	28	
T	29	◐
W	30	
T	31	

SEPTEMBER		
F	1	
S	2	
S	**3**	
M	4	
T	5	
W	6	○
T	7	
F	8	
S	9	
S	**10**	
M	11	
T	12	
W	13	◑
T	14	
F	15	
S	16	
S	**17**	
M	18	
T	19	
W	20	●
T	21	
F	22	
S	23	
S	**24**	
M	25	
T	26	
W	27	◐
T	28	
F	29	
S	30	

OCTOBER		
S	1	
M	2	
T	3	
W	4	
T	5	○
F	6	
S	7	
S	8	
M	9	
T	10	
W	11	
T	12	◑
F	13	
S	14	
S	15	
M	16	
T	17	
W	18	
T	19	●
F	20	
S	21	
S	22	
M	23	
T	24	
W	25	
T	26	
F	27	◐
S	28	
S	29	
M	30	
T	31	

NOVEMBER		
W	1	
T	2	
F	3	
S	4	○
S	5	
M	6	
T	7	
W	8	
T	9	
F	10	◑
S	11	
S	12	
M	13	
T	14	
W	15	
T	16	
F	17	
S	18	●
S	19	
M	20	
T	21	
W	22	
T	23	
F	24	
S	25	
S	26	◐
M	27	
T	28	
W	29	
T	30	

DECEMBER		
F	1	
S	2	
S	3	○
M	4	
T	5	
W	6	
T	7	
F	8	
S	9	
S	10	◑
M	11	
T	12	
W	13	
T	14	
F	15	
S	16	
S	17	
M	18	●
T	19	
W	20	
T	21	
F	22	
S	23	
S	24	
M	25	
T	26	◐
W	27	
T	28	
F	29	
S	30	
S	31	

Stay close to those who are not afraid to be vulnerable,
because they have confidence in themselves and know that,
at some point in our lives, we all stumble;
they do not interpret this as a sign of weakness,
but of humanity.

MANUSCRIPT FOUND IN ACCRA

JANUARY

Tolerance

1 | Sunday

That is why they are warriors of light.
Because they fail. Because they ask questions.
Because they keep looking for a meaning.
And, in the end, they will find it.

MANUAL OF THE WARRIOR OF LIGHT

2 Monday

3 Tuesday

Life is too short, or too long,
for me to allow myself the luxury of living it so badly.

ELEVEN MINUTES

4 Wednesday

5 Thursday

6 | Friday

7 | Saturday

8 | Sunday

Silence does not always mean consent
– it is generally merely our inability to react immediately.

THE DEVIL AND MISS PRYM

9 Monday

10 Tuesday

I'm not tormenting myself.
I learned long ago that in order to heal my wounds,
I must have the courage to face up to them.

ALEPH

11 | Wednesday

12 | Thursday

13 | Friday

14 | Saturday

15 Sunday

All human beings are different and should take their right
to be different to its ultimate consequences.

THE WINNER STANDS ALONE

16 Monday

17 Tuesday

Grace cannot be hoarded.
There are no banks where it can be deposited
to be used when you feel more at peace with yourself.

THE ZAHIR

18 Wednesday

19 Thursday

20 Friday

21 Saturday

2 2 | Sunday

Doubt, far from paralyzing me,
pushed me in the direction of oceans whose very existence
I could not admit.

THE WITCH OF PORTOBELLO

2 3 Monday

2 4 Tuesday

The only way to save our dreams
is by being generous to ourselves.

THE PILGRIMAGE

25 Wednesday

26 Thursday

27 Friday

28 Saturday

29 Sunday

Never stop having doubts.
If you ever do, it will be because you've stopped moving forward.

BRIDA

30 Monday

31 Tuesday

It's a serious illness forcing yourself to be the same
as everyone else...it's a distortion of nature,
it goes against God's laws, for in all the world's woods and forests,
He did not create a single leaf the same as another.

VERONIKA DECIDES TO DIE

FEBRUARY

Affection

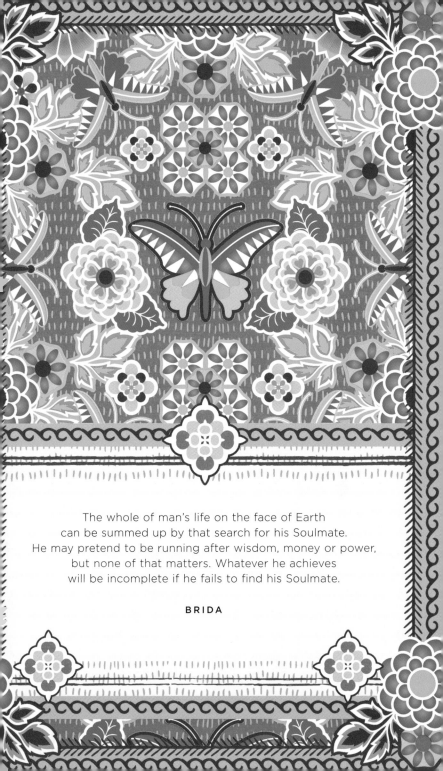

The whole of man's life on the face of Earth
can be summed up by that search for his Soulmate.
He may pretend to be running after wisdom, money or power,
but none of that matters. Whatever he achieves
will be incomplete if he fails to find his Soulmate.

BRIDA

1 Wednesday

2 Thursday

For years, I fought against my heart,
because I was afraid of sadness, suffering, loneliness.
I always knew that real love was above all that
and that it would be better to die than to stop loving.

BY THE RIVER PIEDRA I SAT DOWN AND WEPT

3 Friday

4 Saturday

Life attracts life.

THE ALCHEMIST

5 | Sunday

6 | Monday

7 | Tuesday

8 Wednesday

9 Thursday

The day will come when those knocking at the door will see it open;
those who ask will receive and those who weep will be comforted.

THE VALKYRIES

10 Friday

11 Saturday

Not everyone who owns a pile of gold the size
of that hill to the south of our city is rich.
The truly rich person is the one who is in contact
with the energy of Love every second of his existence.

MANUSCRIPT FOUND IN ACCRA

12 Sunday

13 | Monday

14 | Tuesday

15 Wednesday

16 Thursday

Only true love can withstand separation.

THE WITCH OF PORTOBELLO

17 Friday

18 Saturday

The taste of things recovered
is the sweetest honey we will ever know.

THE ZAHIR

19 Sunday

20 Monday

21 Tuesday

22 | Wednesday

23 | Thursday

Those who have never been wounded by love can never say:
I lived, because they haven't lived.

CHRONICLE: CONVENTION OF THOSE WOUNDED IN LOVE

24 Friday

25 Saturday

Fear makes us ashamed of showing our affection.

BY THE RIVER PIEDRA I SAT DOWN AND WEPT

26 Sunday

27 Monday

28 Tuesday

Stay close to those who allow the light of Love
to shine forth without restrictions, judgments or rewards,
without letting it be blocked by the fear of being misunderstood.

MANUSCRIPT FOUND IN ACCRA

Help us to see in each grain of desert sand
proof of the miracle of difference,
and may that encourage us to accept ourselves as we are.
Because just as no two grains of sand are alike,
so no two human beings will think and act in the same way.

MANUSCRIPT FOUND IN ACCRA

MARCH

Clarity

1 Wednesday

2 Thursday

The warrior has memories too,
but he learns how to separate the useful from the unnecessary;
he disposes of his emotional rubbish.

MANUAL OF THE WARRIOR OF LIGHT

3 Friday

4 Saturday

Love was the key to the understanding of all the mysteries.

BRIDA

5 Sunday

6 | Monday

7 | Tuesday

8 Wednesday

9 Thursday

The path is more important than whatever made you set off along it.

THE WITCH OF PORTOBELLO

10 | Friday

11 | Saturday

The solitude of the desert
can bring us into close contact with the invisible world.

THE VALKYRIES

12 | Sunday

13 | Monday

14 | Tuesday

15 Wednesday

16 Thursday

The second symptom of the death of our dreams are our certainties.
If we look at life like a great adventure to be lived,
we end up thinking we are wise,
just and correct in the little that we ask of existence.

THE PILGRIMAGE

17 Friday

18 Saturday

Know that there's a finish line
and that you can't give up halfway through.

ADULTERY

19 | Sunday

20 Monday

21 Tuesday

22 Wednesday

23 Thursday

All my life I did my best to be a cistern,
never going beyond the limits of my inner walls.

VERONIKA DECIDES TO DIE

24 Friday

25 Saturday

Scars are medals won in a war waged
in the name of faith and dreams.

THE WINNER STANDS ALONE

26 | Sunday

27 Monday

28 Tuesday

29 Wednesday

---

30 Thursday

Remember one thing:
You do not drown simply by plunging into water,
you only drown if you stay beneath the surface.

MANUAL OF THE WARRIOR OF LIGHT

31 Friday

May our eyes open so that we can see
that no two days are ever the same.
Each one brings with it a different miracle,
which allows us to go on breathing,
dreaming and walking in the sun.

MANUSCRIPT FOUND IN ACCRA

APRIL

Cooperation

A warrior does not need to be reminded
of the help given him by others;
he is the first to remember and makes sure
to share with them any rewards he receives.

MANUAL OF THE WARRIOR OF LIGHT

1 | Saturday

2 Sunday

Do one thing: Live the life you always wanted to live.
Avoid criticizing others and concentrate on fulfilling your dreams.
This may not seem very important to you,
but God, who sees all, knows that the example you
give is helping Him to improve the world.
And each day, He will bestow more blessings upon it.

MANUSCRIPT FOUND IN ACCRA

3 Monday

4 Tuesday

The earth produces enough to satisfy need not greed.

THE VALKYRIES

5 Wednesday

6 Thursday

7 Friday

8 Saturday

9 | Sunday

A warrior never gives in to fear when he is searching
for what he needs. Without love, he is nothing.

MANUAL OF THE WARRIOR OF LIGHT

10 Monday

11 Tuesday

Teach those who want to learn.
The reason doesn't matter.

THE WITCH OF PORTOBELLO

12 | Wednesday

13 | Thursday

14 Friday

15 Saturday

16 Sunday

A life without cause is a life without effect.

ALEPH

17 Monday

18 Tuesday

On the road of life,
we will always find hard problems to resolve.

THE PILGRIMAGE

19 Wednesday

20 Thursday

21 Friday

22 Saturday

23 | Sunday

Love is. No definitions.
Love and don't ask too many questions. Just love.

THE WITCH OF PORTOBELLO

24 Monday

25 Tuesday

The Spiritual Quest is made up of constant beginnings,
and the only thing that matters – always – is the desire to carry on.

THE VALKYRIES

26 Wednesday

27 Thursday

28 Friday

29 Saturday

30 | Sunday

Luck is knowing to look around and see where your friends are,
because it is through their words that the angels
are able to make themselves heard.

THE ZAHIR

MAY

Faith

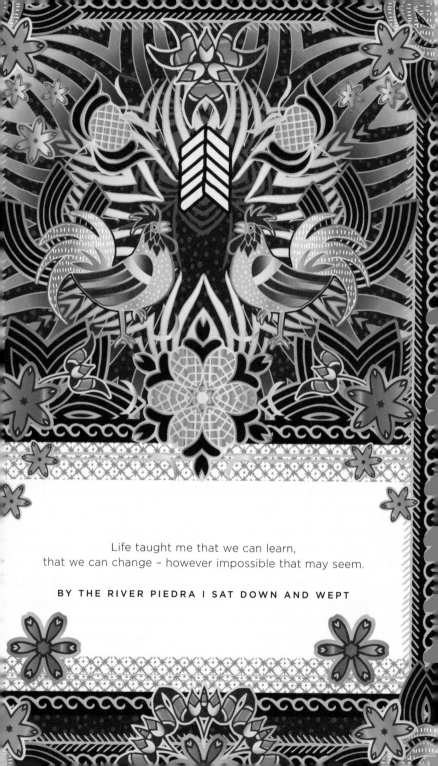

Life taught me that we can learn,
that we can change – however impossible that may seem.

BY THE RIVER PIEDRA I SAT DOWN AND WEPT

1 | Monday

2 | Tuesday

3 Wednesday

4 Thursday

Our one true choice is to plunge
into the mystery of that uncontrollable force.
We could say: 'I've suffered greatly before
and I know that this won't last either'
and thus drive Love from our door,
but if we did that, we would become dead to life.

M A N U S C R I P T   F O U N D   I N   A C C R A

5 | Friday

6 | Saturday

The greatest thing a human being can do is to accept the Mystery.

BRIDA

7 | Sunday

8 | Monday

9 | Tuesday

10 | Wednesday

11 | Thursday

Faith is not desire. Faith is Will. Will is a force.

THE WITCH OF PORTOBELLO

12 Friday

13 Saturday

I must accept the blessings of today in order to create what I have;
if I do this with detachment and without guilt,
tomorrow I will receive more blessings.

CHRONICLE: BETWEEN EKATERINHURG AND NOVOSIBIRSK

14 | Sunday

15 Monday

16 Tuesday

17 Wednesday

18 Thursday

There are times when we must accept the mystery
and understand that each of us has a gift. Some know how to heal,
others have wise words, others can speak with the spirits.

THE VALKYRIES

19 Friday

20 Saturday

Let us plunge together then down the dangerous path of surrender.
It may be dangerous, but it is the only path worth following.

MANUSCRIPT FOUND IN ACCRA

21 | Sunday

2 2 Monday

2 3 Tuesday

24 Wednesday

25 Thursday

You do not need to move mountains in order to prove your faith.

BY THE RIVER PIEDRA I SAT DOWN AND WEPT

26 | Friday

27 | Saturday

There are times when God demands obedience,
but there there are also times when he wants to test our will
and challenge us to understand His love.

THE FIFTH MOUNTAIN

28 Sunday

29 | Monday

30 | Tuesday

31 Wednesday

God is not revenge, God is Love.
His only punishment consists in forcing someone
who interrupted some labor of Love to continue it.

THE PILGRIMAGE

When they ask, do not forget to give.
When they knock at your door, be sure to open it.
When they lose something and come to you,
do whatever you can to help them find what they have lost.

ALEPH

JUNE

Friendship

1 Thursday

Friendship is one of the many faces of Love,
and Love is not swayed by opinions;
Love accepts its companion unconditionally
and allows each to grow in his or her own way.

MANUSCRIPT FOUND IN ACCRA

2 Friday

3 Saturday

During the very worst crisis of my life,
friends came to my aid.
Ever since then, the first thing I do is to ask for help.

CHRONICLE: THE CRISIS AND ITS TRAPS

4 | Sunday

5 | Monday

6 | Tuesday

7 | Wednesday

8 | Thursday

Life sometimes separates people so that
they can realize how much they mean to each other.

THE WINNER STANDS ALONE

9 Friday

10 Saturday

Loyalty can never be imposed by force, fear, insecurity, or intimidation.
It is a choice that only strong spirits have the courage to make.
And because it is a choice, it will never tolerate betrayal,
but will always be generous with mistakes.

MANUSCRIPT FOUND IN ACCRA

11 | Sunday

12 Monday

13 Tuesday

14 Wednesday

15 Thursday

In order to have faith in your own path,
you do not need to prove that someone else's path is wrong.

MANUAL OF THE WARRIOR OF LIGHT

16 Friday

17 Saturday

If there's love enough amongst you, you'll have an abundant harvest,
because love is the feeling that transforms everything.

THE WITCH OF PORTOBELLO

18 | Sunday

19 Monday

20 Tuesday

21 Wednesday

22 Thursday

There is always someone waiting for their special person,
whether in the middle of the desert or in the middle of a great city.

THE ALCHEMIST

23 | Friday

24 | Saturday

If you love someone, then you want your beloved to be happy.
You might feel frightened for him initially,
but that feeling soon gives way to pride at seeing him
doing what he wants to do,
and going where he always dreamed of going.

MANUSCRIPT FOUND IN ACCRA

2 5 | Sunday

26 Monday

27 Tuesday

28 Wednesday

29 Thursday

Everything should be a personal manifestation
of our will to fight the Good Fight. Otherwise,
if we fail to realize that we need everyone and everything,
we will be arrogant warriors.

THE PILGRIMAGE

30 Friday

Remember: never be arrogant with the humble,
and never be humble with the arrogant.

CHRONICLE: STORIES ABOUT ARROGANCE

JULY

Love in Motion

What we need to learn is always there before us,
we just have to look around us with respect and attention
in order to discover where God is leading us.

THE ZAHIR

1 | Saturday

2 Sunday

People have been trying to understand
the universe through love ever since the beginning of time.

BRIDA

3 Monday

4 Tuesday

The angels are love in motion, which never stops,
but struggles to grow, and is beyond good and evil.

THE VALKYRIES

5 Wednesday

6 Thursday

7 Friday

8 Saturday

9 Sunday

The warrior fights the Good Fight and helps others,
even though he does not quite understand why.

MANUAL OF THE WARRIOR OF LIGHT

10 Monday

11 Tuesday

Love does not ask many questions,
because if we begin to think,
we begin to feel afraid.

BY THE RIVER PIEDRA I SAT DOWN AND WEPT

12 | Wednesday

13 | Thursday

14 | Friday

15 | Saturday

16 | Sunday

Along with the birth of love came a need
to find an answer to the mystery of existence.

ALEPH

17 Monday

18 Tuesday

The essence of life is the ability to love.

THE WINNER STANDS ALONE

19 | Wednesday

20 | Thursday

21 | Friday

22 | Saturday

23 | Sunday

When you love each other, you have to be ready for anything.
Because love is like a kaleidoscope,
the kind we used to play with when we were kids.
It's in constant movement and never repeats itself.

ADULTERY

24 Monday

25 Tuesday

Love is neither large nor small, it is simply love.

26 | Wednesday

27 | Thursday

2 8 | Friday

2 9 | Saturday

30 Sunday

31 Monday

Why are people unhappy?
Because they want to imprison the energy of love,
which is impossible.

THE ZAHIR

When someone is looking for his Personal Legend,
the Universe does everything
it can to help that person find what he desires.

THE ALCHEMIST

AUGUST

Understanding

---

1 | Tuesday

2 Wednesday

3 Thursday

For the warrior, there is no 'better' or 'worse':
everyone has the necessary gifts for his particular path.

MANUAL OF THE WARRIOR OF LIGHT

4 Friday

5 Saturday

The path of wisdom means not being afraid to make mistakes.

BRIDA

6 | Sunday

7 | Monday

8 | Tuesday

9 Wednesday

10 Thursday

All men go through stages, which they must see through to the end.
However, they must not confuse those stages
with the reason for their existence.

THE FIFTH MOUNTAIN

11 Friday

12 Saturday

Although we cannot control God's time,
it is part of the human condition to want to receive the thing
we are waiting for as quickly as possible.

MANUSCRIPT FOUND IN ACCRA

13 | Sunday

14 Monday

15 Tuesday

16 Wednesday

17 Thursday

It is one thing for the whole universe
to conspire to make our dreams come true,
it is quite another to set oneself entirely unnecessary challenges.

CHRONICLE: THE BLIND MAN AND EVEREST

18 Friday

19 Saturday

Sometimes you have to travel a long way to find what is near.

A L E P H

20 Sunday

21 Monday

22 Tuesday

23 | Wednesday

24 | Thursday

The Will was the main target of Bitterness.
People afflicted by this malaise gradually lost
the will to do anything and, within a few years,
were unable to escape from their only little world.

VERONIKA DECIDES TO DIE

2 5 Friday

2 6 Saturday

The truth is that all problems seem very simple
once they have been resolved. The great victory,
which appears so simple today,
was the result of a series of small victories that went unnoticed.

MANUAL OF THE WARRIOR OF LIGHT

27 | Sunday

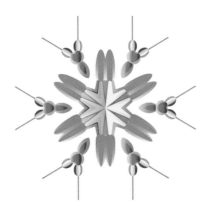

28 | Monday

29 | Tuesday

30 Wednesday

31 Thursday

There is no such thing as a 'one and only chance';
life always gives you another chance.

THE WINNER STANDS ALONE

SEPTEMBER

Dignity

Carry in your memory, for the rest of your life,
the good things that came out of those difficulties.
They will serve as a proof of your abilities
and will give you confidence
when you are faced by other obstacles.

MANUAL OF THE WARRIOR OF LIGHT

1 Friday

2 Saturday

3 Sunday

The people who really help others are not trying to be useful,
but are simply leading a useful life.
They rarely give advice, but serve as an example.

MANUSCRIPT FOUND IN ACCRA

4 Monday

5 Tuesday

Wisdom is only valuable if it helps you
to overcome some obstacle.

THE PILGRIMAGE

6 | Wednesday

7 | Thursday

8 Friday

9 Saturday

10 Sunday

Talent is a universal gift,
but it takes a lot of courage to use it.
Don't be afraid to be the best.

THE WINNER STANDS ALONE

11 | Monday

12 | Tuesday

If I must be faithful to someone or something,
then I have, first of all, to be faithful to myself.

ELEVEN MINUTES

13 Wednesday

14 Thursday

15 Friday

16 Saturday

17 | Sunday

The warrior prefers the taste of struggle
and the excitement of the unknown.

THE ALCHEMIST

18 Monday

19 Tuesday

Free will demands immense responsibility;
it is hard work, and brings with it anguish and suffering.

THE WITCH OF PORTOBELLO

20 | Wednesday

21 | Thursday

22 Friday

23 Saturday

24 Sunday

A warrior of light dances with his companions,
but does not place the responsibility for his actions on anyone else.

MANUAL OF THE WARRIOR OF LIGHT

25 Monday

26 Tuesday

The strong are generous in victory.

MANUSCRIPT FOUND IN ACCRA

27 | Wednesday

28 | Thursday

29 Friday

30 Saturday

My path exists, and I do whatever
I can to travel that path with dignity.
What is that path? It is the path of someone looking for love.

BY THE RIVER PIEDRA I SAT DOWN AND WEPT

Friendship is like a river; it flows around rocks,
adapts itself to valleys and mountains,
occasionally turns into a pool until the hollow
in the ground is full and it can continue on its way.

MANUSCRIPT FOUND IN ACCRA

OCTOBER

Delicacy

1 Sunday

The warrior views life with tenderness and determination.

MANUAL OF THE WARRIOR OF LIGHT

2 Monday

3 Tuesday

An embrace means: I don't feel threatened by you;
I'm not afraid to be this close; I can relax, feel at home,
feel protected and in the presence of someone who understands me.

ALEPH

4 Wednesday

5 Thursday

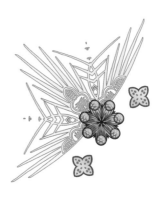

6 Friday

7 Saturday

8 | Sunday

Arrogance causes us to humiliate our fellow man or woman.
Elegance teaches us to walk in the light.

MANUSCRIPT FOUND IN ACCRA

9 | Monday

10 | Tuesday

Lord, allow us, through work and Action,
to share a little of the love we receive.

CHRONICLE: THE PRAYER I FORGOT

11 Wednesday

12 Thursday

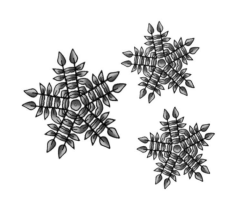

13 | Friday

14 | Saturday

15 Sunday

I am spreading the energy of love all around me;
it is more powerful than the forces of darkness.

THE WINNER STANDS ALONE

OCTOBER

Week 42

16 Monday

17 Tuesday

Help me to be humble enough to accept that I am no different
from other people.

BRIDA

18 | Wednesday

19 | Thursday

20 Friday

21 Saturday

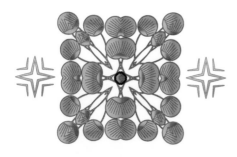

22 Sunday

Of all the powerful weapons of destruction man has invented,
the most terrible – and the most cowardly – is the word.

CHRONICLE: NOTES FROM MY NON-EXISTENT DIARY

23 Monday

24 Tuesday

When we are walking our chosen path,
we walk elegantly, emanating light.

MANUSCRIPT FOUND IN ACCRA

25 | Wednesday

26 | Thursday

27 Friday

28 Saturday

29 Sunday

When we discard the superfluous, we discover simplicity
and concentration, and the simpler and more sober our posture,
the more beautiful it will be, even if, initially, it feels awkward.

THE WITCH OF PORTOBELLO

30 Monday

31 Tuesday

But every tribe, every people, has values that they associate
with elegance: hospitality, respect, good manners.

MANUSCRIPT FOUND IN ACCRA

NOVEMBER

Happiness

Anyone wishing to fight the Good Fight must look at
the world as if it were a great treasure,
which is there waiting to be discovered and conquered.

THE PILGRIMAGE

1 Wednesday

2 Thursday

Love is only a word,
until we decide to let it possess us with all its force.

MANUSCRIPT FOUND IN ACCRA

3 Friday

4 Saturday

There is nothing wrong with doing simple things.

THE WITCH OF PORTOBELLO

5 | Sunday

6 | Monday

7 | Tuesday

8 Wednesday

9 Thursday

Take pleasure in love.
Take pleasure in victory.
Follow your heart.

THE VALKYRIES

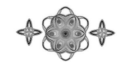

10 Friday

11 Saturday

Every morning carries within it a hidden miracle
and we need to find that miracle.

CHRONICLE: RESPECTING WORK

12 | Sunday

13 Monday

14 Tuesday

15 Wednesday

16 Thursday

If you want to see a rainbow you have to learn to like the rain.

ALEPH

17 Friday

18 Saturday

Even if he is not in the mood,
the warrior of light tries to enjoy the small everyday things of life.

MANUAL OF THE WARRIOR OF LIGHT

19 | Sunday

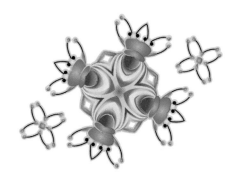

20 Monday

21 Tuesday

22 Wednesday

---

23 Thursday

If you believe in victory, then victory will believe in you.

THE WINNER STANDS ALONE

24 Friday

25 Saturday

The Path of Peace appears to be a fight, but it isn't.
It's the art of filling up what is missing
and emptying out what is superfluous.

ALEPH

26 | Sunday

27 Monday

28 Tuesday

29 Wednesday

30 Thursday

Each day carries within it a hidden blessing,
a blessing that is only valid for that day
and cannot be stored away or hidden.

CHRONICLE: CONVERSATIONS WITH THE MASTER

Let us first seek Love,
and everything else will be added.

ADULTERY

DECEMBER

Empathy

1 Friday

2 Saturday

The warrior respects the suffering of others
and does not try to compare it with his own.

MANUAL OF THE WARRIOR OF LIGHT

3 | Sunday

4 Monday

5 Tuesday

6 | Wednesday

7 | Thursday

At the first sign of indifference or lack of enthusiasm
towards other people, take note! The only preventative against
this disease is the realization that the soul suffers, suffers greatly,
when we force it to live superficially.
The soul loves all things beautiful and deep.

THE WINNER STANDS ALONE

8 | Friday

9 | Saturday

The universe always helps us to fight for our dreams,
however foolish they may seem.

BY THE RIVER PIEDRA I SAT DOWN AND WEPT

10 Sunday

11 Monday

12 Tuesday

13 Wednesday

14 Thursday

Love is sharing the world with someone else.

THE VALKYRIES

15 Friday

16 Saturday

Walk with a firm and joyful step, unafraid of stumbling.
All movements are accompanied by their allies,
who will help whenever necessary.

CHRONICLE: ON ELEGANCE

17 | Sunday

18 Monday

19 Tuesday

20 | Wednesday

21 | Thursday

Angels are visible to those who accept the light
and break their agreement with the dark.

THE VALKYRIES

22 | Friday

23 | Saturday

Anyone who falls in love without taking
into account the common good will be condemned
to live in constant fear of hurting his partner,
of irritating his new love, of losing everything he built.

THE WITCH OF PORTOBELLO

24 | Sunday

25 Monday

26 Tuesday

27 | Wednesday

28 | Thursday

Love justifies certain acts that mere human beings cannot understand,
unless they happen to be experiencing
what that other person has experienced.

THE WINNER STANDS ALONE

29 Friday

30 Saturday

Is it possible to know something without ever having experienced it?
Yes, but it will never truly be part of you.

ALEPH

31 | Sunday

Also by Paulo Coelho

THE PILGRIMAGE

THE ALCHEMIST

BRIDA

THE VALKYRIES

BY THE RIVER PIEDRA I SAT DOWN AND WEPT

THE FIFTH MOUNTAIN

WARRIOR OF THE LIGHT

VERONIKA DECIDES TO DIE

THE DEVIL AND MISS PRYM

ELEVEN MINUTES

THE ZAHIR

LIKE THE FLOWING RIVER

THE WITCH OF PORTOBELLO

THE WINNER STANDS ALONE

ALEPH

MANUSCRIPT FOUND IN ACCRA

ADULTERY

Original title: *Amizade 2017*

Copyright © 2016 Paulo Coelho and Forlagshuset Bazar AS
http://paulocoelhoblog.com/

Published by arrangement with Sant Jordi Asociados, Agencia Literaria, S.L.U.,
Barcelona (Spain). www.santjordi-asociados.com

All rights reserved. Published in the United States of America by Vintage Books,
a division of Penguin Random House LLC, New York, and in Canada by Random House
of Canada Ltd., Toronto, Penguin Random House Companies.

Vintage is a registered trademark and Vintage International and the colophon
are trademarks of Penguin Random House LLC.

Vintage ISBN: 978-1-101-97264-9

Quote selection: Márcia Botelho
Translation copyright © Margaret Jull Costa
Illustrations by Catalina Estrada, www.catalinaestrada.com
Author photograph © Paul Macleod
Design by Lene Stangebye Geving / Mercè Roig

www.vintagebooks.com

Printed and bound by TBB, Eslovaquia, 2016